Poetic Meditations for the Evolutionary Journey

D1730821

Also by Anjali Soi

Poetic Meditations for the Astrological Journey —
Adult Coloring Book

Velvet Evenings — A Poetry Collection

Explore the signs of the zodiac in
Evolutionary Astrology

Poetic Meditations for the Evolutionary Journey

Anjali Soi

avabhAsana Arts

copyright © Anjali Soi, 2022
All Rights Reserved

www.anjalisoi.com

ISBN-13: 979-8832964478   Printed in the United States of America

ATTENTION: ORGANIZATIONS AND BUSINESSES
This book is available at quantity discounts with bulk purchase for educational, nonprofit or business use. For information, please email Anjali Soi at anjalisoi@gmail.com.

Contents

Introduction

This book provides meditations and poetry to help you learn the nature of all twelve signs of the zodiac beginning in Aries and ending in Pisces. Evolutionary astrology believes Pluto is the Soul and the path of evolution, embodied by the meaning of Scorpio and the 8th house.

Pluto is the Soul's Unconscious desires and each sign represents a certain aspect of the human life and psyche on the earth plane. The sign is a sub-journey in the entire human journey represented by the twelve signs. The Plutonian theme of birth, death and transformation is alive throughout the zodiacal journey.

Each sign is introduced with its' basic elemental qualities. It is yin or yang, fire, earth, air or water and cardinal, fixed or mutable. Cardinal is an initiating quality while fixed is firmly set and mutable is adjusting. The evolutionary lessons for each sign are provided as 'Evolutionary Goals' along with archetypes, topics and traits.

The sun sign dates are not included because the essential nature of each sign is described no matter what planet transits it on the date of birth. You will obviously have a certain analysis depending on the planet transiting a sign but the focus of this book is only on the *sign's* meaning.

I hope you find this collection to be helpful whether you are a beginner to astrology or an advanced learner. Use it as a learning aid or meditative guide as you explore the human personality through the lens of evolution.

Aries ♈

Nature – Yang, Fire, Cardinal
Ruler – Mars, 1st house
Archetypes – Warrior, Soldier, Hero/Heroine, Pioneer, Boxer

Evolutionary Goals:
- Awareness of conscious desires
- Independence
- Self-discovery and self-assertion

Topics: primal nature, instincts, will, separation

Traits: courageous, competitive, aggressive, wild, impatient, impulsive, reckless, rageful

Aries Meditation

I fell out of the womb saying "here I am!" grabbing at ears and eyes and 'ahhhing' at the walls around me.

I dropped my toys to hear the 'crash' they made and eventually battled with my playground mates, pushing them off the monkey bars.

I wanted to swing with reckless abandon after all.

Restless, I snatched my sword and ventured into the forest, slashing at leaping wolves and lurking jaguars.

I caught fish when hungry and ate nuts found under some leaves.

My footsteps eventually carried me to a cliff's border where I saw how far they pioneered a path.

The prowling wolves and bobcats did not disturb my ambition.

They did not trap me in their prowling growls or schemes.

I did not let the scorpions sting or the alligators chomp me apart.

Instead my aspirations were revealed, my Self-hood realized.

Identity

The arrow's aim is the only object of my eye.

I sense the fear, thick like a massive black hole suffocating me in its' core.

My spear can hardly pierce it. But my arrow never quivers.

A flame within me will not succumb to the terror. Courage rages within me.

I will triumph because there is never another choice.

This is who I am. This is how I war.

Rawed

No I will not curb my craving.
I am not a stone.

There are veins in my leaves.

If you struggle with loss, go somewhere else.

Only desire here, only urges.

Where is fury these days? Why is there such caution?

The sexes of men wobble.

Where is life for a human Rawed.

Taurus ♉

Nature — Yin, Earth, Fixed
Ruler — Venus, 2nd house
Archetypes — Builder, Entrepreneur, Gardener, Material
Artist, Bully

Evolutionary Goals:
- Self-reliance
- Self-sufficiency
- Awareness of needs and values

Topics: survival, resources, security, stability, cultivation

Traits: determined, resilient, patient, integrous, cautious, possessive, stubborn, indulgent

Taurus Meditation

What makes a rock, a rock? a stem, a stem?
blooming tomato?

What makes them what they are?

Maybe it is the rock's outline that makes its' form. A boundary must define one from another after all.

How else will one know what one is? How else will one know its' worth?

Yet though they exist apart, the rock, stem and tomato are connected. They share a bond.

Surviving in the same dirt, they comfort one another in sadness and pleasure, remaining as one foundation whether blooming or stagnant.

Sitting by the hearth, I'm wrapped in warmth and in the grasp of their protection.

I may have trouble leaving their hold as I travel from place to place but we feel satisfied knowing they are the ground I walk on.

I continue to dig this precious dirt with my bare hands, knowing I am sustained not only within myself but together with what grows.

The Mountain Climb

Climbing a mountain might seem incredibly challenging at first. You wonder: how will I climb such steep slopes or get over sharp angles? What if a big boulder slides down and smushes me to smithereens? My shoes might tear or I'll break a bone. What if I can't find anything to eat after finishing the granola bars in my backpack? What if I die?

Well, first you have to decide if you want to even climb this mountain. Is it worth the risk? Yes or no. You have five seconds to decide. Go: one…two…three…four…five. If you chose yes, read on. If no, God help you.

Now that we know for sure you want to climb the mountain, you must take the first step according to a famous Chinese proverb. So here we go. Right, left, right, left. We already took four steps to the base of the mountain! By the way, I hope you brought lots of pairs of dry socks. Wet, muddy socks are no good on a climb. I'm also assuming you have somewhat of a basic skill set in mountain climbing. This is all metaphoric of course.

You will also need tools like maps, pens, compasses, sharp sticks to clear away brush, a feel for the inclines and a sharp eye for animals who might not like you. Your minds will have to be alert and your muscles strong. Don't forget the insect repellant.

Next we must be determined and focused. You can't keep complaining about the worms climbing up your leg or the ants in your sleeping bag. This is about survival. Don't get frustrated, give up and go back to the bottom. Whether it takes you five days or five years, you must complete the task.

This journey will require a lot of patience. There will be a lot of work to do but times of rest, reflection and periods of waiting, of literally watching the clouds go by, will exist. You may need to cross a mountain pass but a herd of mountain goats might not let you through. You can say 'shoo' all you want but they may not budge so just make a polite request. You might as well enjoy the break and take a nap or sing a mountain song of some kind while you wait.

You should also know you can't take anything that isn't yours. Like you might see berries hidden under some leaves. If you want them, make sure those berries are for the general public. If there's a bunch of berries say by a tree covered under leaves, an animal probably stored them there. You probably can't have them. Even if you feel like you would really appreciate and enjoy them, don't take them.

The last thing to remember is you must be willing to defend and walk the mountain at all cost. You might lose everything and everyone. Be tough. Don't let disappointments and hurdles discourage you. It won't be long before you get to enjoy the Mountain View.

Gemini ♊

Nature – Yang, Air, Mutable
Ruler – Mercury, 3rd house
Archetypes – Messenger, Writer, Educator, Magician, Twin

Evolutionary Goals:
- Experience diversity and variety of phenomena
- Make links and connections
- Communication and thought

Topics: left-brain, logic, intellect, facts, early learning, siblings, local travel and environment

Traits: versatile, quick-witted, flexible, clever, anxious, scatterbrained, superficial, never has enough information

Gemini Meditation

I explore thought,
shapes shifting into form,
strange yet ingenious.

Polarity synthesizes,
movement comes easily.

Restlessness relieves,
more forms emerge.

I move with the turns.

Then words appear as if
designed by magic.

Curious, I search for more
shapes to find and tell,

diverse thoughts to
grab and mold.

The Kids' Section in the Library

I'm in the children's section of the library hoping I don't get
kicked out for being over twelve. I'd rather sit with the kids.
The computer wasn't working but the librarian came over and
fixed it. I felt a bit self-conscious knowing she had to help an
overweight Indian woman sitting in the midst of human beings
less than four feet tall but I had no choice. I thanked her for
letting me sit there. If I sit in the adult section, I might die from
boredom aka the real world. Plus little kids' conversations are
mad entertaining.

The library is an interesting place during the summer. The
rules of quietude and silence no longer apply. Two-year olds
march around screaming their heads off while people are
trying to work. But I love it. I don't mind being interrupted by
cute little humans that lighten your heart for some time even if
piercingly.

I also don't mind being 'interrupted' by this little girl sitting at the computer across from me, asking her brother lots of questions in a high-pitched, screeching voice. Adorable. How could you not sit with the kids? How could you not want to be around life all the time?

She just asked her brother how she can become a mommy. Her brother said she can't! She asks 'why not?' And persists.

Oh no, her brother farted!

A Reflection

My intellect is still like clear, cool waters.
It holds mirrors that reflect to you who you are.

So you choose what you are, you choose what you want me to be.

Cancer ♋

Nature — Yin, Water, Cardinal
Ruler — Moon, 4th house
Archetypes — Protector, Nurturer, Caregiver, Counselor,
Mother

Evolutionary Goals:
- Feel emotions and meet own emotional needs
- Develop subjective consciousness
- Develop internal security

Topics: emotional body, feelings, preservation instinct, self-care, home

Traits: sensitive, vulnerable, caring, gentle, immature, insecure, needy, moody

Cancer Meditation

I am water, but not like the deep ocean or an immense glacier.

I am a stream, a river of eternal instincts and emotions that overflow onto the riverbanks.

Who will calm me?

What will quell my river waves?

Is it the bedrock that will soothe me? Will it

quench my inner thirst?

Or the small campfire close by?

Maybe the breezes circling me above?

I need eagerly but nothing relieves me.

My feeling is forever, my cup remains empty.

La Loba

I am La Loba.
I arrive in the midst of a Soul's drought.

The lost wake from humble slumber,
I shake their Spirits to venture out.

I howl to life a powerful wolf,
the slithers of sandy rattlesnakes.

What creatures are you looking for?
Their skeletons lie in a desert cave.

I sing, I scream, I roam, I moan,
the wolf leaps up and over the mound.

An onyx crow lands far below and
caws a haunting, savage sound.

Rain

I am Demeter.

I am Rudaali.

I am a Womb who grieves a loss so big, its' grief I cannot contain in my body.

I yell, I tantrum, I nurture, I ache.

I laugh and I cry.

And then I walk in the Rain. I walk in the Rain.

Leo ♌

Nature — Yang, Fire, Fixed
Ruler — Sun, 5th house
Archetypes — Performer, Child, Entertainer, King/Queen, Lover

Evolutionary Goals:
- Creative self-actualization
- Manifest special purpose and destiny

Topics: creative instincts, children, fun, entertainment, romance

Traits: bold, expressive, energetic, daring, dramatic, arrogant, attention-needy, narcissistic

Leo Meditation

I love to create a story, enact a drama and express myself under the royal hues of the beams.

A child, I leap into the far corners of the stage, this playground I find myself in.

Look at me!

I'm drawing constellations in the sky and painting galaxies!

I'm zooming over planets and speeding through starry hoops!

I'm in the jungle now, spreading my bright blue peacock feathers as I stand on my lion's back.

My joy is hard to contain but why should I?

The audience loves my performance.

You adore me and my purpose is to be on stage.

The Empress

I'm the fire. I'm the pride. I'm the party. I'm the high.

I'm the Diva. I'm the Queen. I'm the lipstick. I'm the need.

I'm the story. I'm the play. I'm the joker. Hear me say.

Bring me dinner. Bring me green. Bring my robes. Leave.

Pink roses

Poetry and chocolates.
Mascara and cologne.

Bubble baths, necklaces,
petals and prosecco.

Cushions and buttons.

Sapphires and bows.

Picnics and sushi.
Evenings so mellow.

Virgo ♍

Nature — Yin, Earth, Mutable
Ruler — Mercury, 6th house
Archetypes — Healer, Servant, Priestess, Employee, Victim

Evolutionary Goals:
- Self-improvement and self-analysis
- Learn healthy discrimination and humility
- Function within a whole

Topics: ego purification, service, routines, health, work

Traits: humble, organized, sacrificial, critical, perfectionist, nit-picky, workaholic, saboteur

Virgo Meditation

I sit at my desk, critical of myself because everything has to be perfect.

The details must be in order, and if they're not, I analyze everything to make it right.

In a constant loop, my mind succumbs to disease, unable to function as required.

Staring out the window, I suddenly notice people walking together, wearing outfits that are simple and charming, almost monastic.

They share smiles that make my 'work' and 'despair' seem futile, insane.

I suddenly feel drawn to walk with them, possibly towards an alternate perfection, one I can't fathom yet.

Can I find hope in this turmoil?

I might be able to redirect my thoughts, even Surrender.

Keeper of the Flame

Do you see this flame I carry in my hands?

Do you see the fire that rises from the center of my palms?

This is Light in my hands. I only hold the Light.

I do nothing else.

My hands cannot hold swords or daggers, pens or weapons while I hold this Light.

I am occupied all day and all night holding this Light.

Even if you come at it, you will not be able to destroy it. A knife cannot slash this flame.

You cannot murder it.

This is Light in my hands.

I only Serve the Light.

Libra ♎

Nature — Yang, Air, Cardinal
Ruler — Venus, 7th house
Archetypes — Artist, Diplomat, Negotiator, Lawyer, Socialite

<u>Evolutionary Goals</u>:
- Balance and equality
- Learn about self through relationships
- Awareness of others

Topics: arts, justice, reconciliation, partnership, beauty

Traits: collaborative, fair, intellectual, sees all sides, codependent, extreme, naïve, indecisive

<u>Libra Meditation</u>

Tornadoes whirl within me.

I slide from one end of the seesaw to the other in turbulence.

I'm ravaged by the winds and can't find grace.

They push me off as I reach for someone to take me to equal ground.

Someone finally comes along and shares a
dance with me,

a beautiful piece of artistry that helps me harness the winds.

The ravaged parts of myself become a symmetry, an elegance I couldn't possibly have found myself.

The tornadoes become breezes and I flutter in flight, gliding along the winds like a hawk in harmony.

I want to dance with my friend for as long as I can, this ally who shared finesse with me,

this partner who listened to me and took me to myself, to brilliance.

An Artist's Life

I am the picture with which you see yourself.

I am the brush that lights your mind.

Justice

Justice isn't delivered in the Courts.
Justice isn't delivered in Temples or Churches.
Justice is certainly not delivered with your ego.

The Universe Delivers Her Justice.

You will bow down to the Universe.

We will bow together.

Scorpio ♏

Nature — Yin, Water, Fixed
Ruler — Pluto, 8th house
Archetypes — Detective, Astrologer, Alchemist, Prostitute, Transformer

Evolutionary Goals:
- Evolve your Unconscious desires
- Power, growth and meaning
- Transformation and metamorphosis
- Awareness of larger forces in the universe

Topics: psyche, power struggles, crisis, conflict, intimacy, marriage, shared resources, deepest attachments, wealth, slavery, debt, sex, regeneration

Traits: profound, probing, psychic, intense, controlling, manipulative, jealous, vindictive

Scorpio Meditation

I do not strive for great heights or open spaces, vast skies or giant mountaintops.

My striving is in the depths, in dark holes and ocean caves where mysteries reveal and obsessions take over.

Here, I discover gems, rocks that seem like planets of knowing that form my Soul. And I find other Souls.

Still, like a caterpillar stuck in a cocoon, I collapse upon myself over and again, struggling to appear.

How will my delicate wings emerge? The pressure is unimaginable.

Am I safe where I am headed? How will I destroy what no longer serves me?

I'm finally forced from this tiny web of strings, a black and violet butterfly,

a final symbol of Power, my existence no longer a secret,

whose meaningful journey sheds tears through which everyone's light is reflected.

Tower

Let yourself fall apart.

Once the tower has crashed, you cannot put the debris back together again.

Give me your fear

Give me more darkness. Give it to me. Give me your garbage. Give me your hate. Give me all that is ugly, the lack, the invisible.

Because I will transform it.

More evil coming at me — more Light.

Tempestuous Throes

Yearning floods me with such vigor yet
I dare not feed the soul to swords.

Tempestuous throes beckon my surrender but
I keep guard near the gates of my heart.

Desire struggles to keep her blaze at bay.
Omens are watched for along the way.

Such feverish urges tempt my torrid mind but
Each craving is relished with warning.

Sagittarius ♐

Nature – Yang, Fire, Mutable
Ruler – Jupiter, 9th house
Archetypes – Explorer, Teacher, Storyteller, Nomad/Gypsy, Journalist

Evolutionary Goals:
- Discovery of truth, beliefs, principles and natural law
- Develop intuition
- Metaphysical awareness

Topics: right brain, interpretation, philosophy, metaphysics, higher education, long-distance travel and experience, media

Traits: optimist, generous, lighthearted, humorous, self-righteous, lying, excessive, Polyanna

Sagittarius Meditation

My gaze falls on the hilltops at the trees lined in rows, the flowers blooming in full with extraordinary colors.

It's as if this view teaches me a wisdom, some law of nature on how to exist, a reason to be.

The birdsong melodies guide my knowing, the owl's hoot my experience of what is.

My faith becomes inspired.

It brightens and becomes red like the ruby hues of the cardinal landing on the branch above me.

I will teach this knowledge to those who seek, those who might perceive their sorrows with smiles if not humor.

Even the gurgling stream giggles as it splashes and splays against the stones.

The owls smile as they watch the otters chase each other in the water.

It's as if some riddle has been solved, a joke relieved.

A nomad, I move on to the next Mountain View.

Perspective

All we ever have is this moment.

All we ever have is the now.

No past or future exists. It is all in our mind.

I stand at the top of the mountain NOW.

I have always made it to my Victory.

As I look below at the valley that nested my voyage, with all its horrors and crazy creatures running about, I wonder how did I ever cross it?

Did it really exist?

This valley I crossed — it isn't there anymore is it?

Capricorn ♑

Nature — Yin, Earth, Cardinal
Ruler — Saturn, 10th house
Archetypes — Authority, Elder, Father, Leader, Dictator

Evolutionary Goals:
- Awareness of time/space reality
- Experience karma
- Learn about personal and other limitations

Topics: career, social role, the past, structures, systems, rules, standards

Traits: practical, disciplined, responsible, committed, rigid, brutal, cold, melancholic

Capricorn Meditation

Stolid chunks of concrete surround me.

Bricks of authority and responsibility, stones of learning and worship, masses of all kinds exist wherever I go.

I lead within these structures with as much dedication as I can.

I uphold principles and make sacrifices along the way.

Often swallowed by a swamp of duty, I'm unaware of my feelings, even that they exist, amidst all purposes.

Stress shudders my bones, a warehouse of frustration and tear.

My spine has become one of those marble pillars I uphold, rigid and immobile,

a splendid image of sophistication but cold and brutalized inside.

Somehow the realization sets in that this pillar is not eternal.

It ends at some point so maybe my spine has limits. Maybe it should stop at some absolute.

I must be diligent but not so serious that I lose sight of the borders.

Petty Tyrant

ruler of egos.
builder of debris,

toppling from
petty needs.

collector of despots,
twists innocence into guilt.

avoids hard work.
obsessed with ease.

loveless.
undignified.
powerless.
blind.

deranged.

Aquarius ♒

Nature — Yang, Air, Fixed
Ruler — Uranus, 11th house
Archetypes — Rebel, Humanitarian, Innovator, Networker,
Friend

Evolutionary Goals:
- Connect with own individuality and authenticity
- Liberate self from conditioning
- Form like-minded associations and objectivity

Topics: inner genius, invention, long-term memory, the future, technology, trauma, new vs. old, networks

Traits: progressive, unique, eccentric, idealistic, radical, aloof, extremist, inflexible

Aquarius Meditation

An icicle fell and hit the side of my head, fracturing my skull into dots.

It's like an electric sword struck me and showed me epiphanies.

I suddenly want to liberate myself from the chains of this world, to help humanize and reform, not isolate and terrorize.

Every morning can no longer be a sunrise that suffers.

The nuisance must be ripped out.

My fellow anguished, let's form deviations around what to annihilate.

Our insights must untwist the chains that exist to reveal each individual.

The inner essence of each member of our tribe must be allowed to shine.

We may have to repair with the very stones we want shattered but let us work to illuminate the authenticity of our vision.

Change

The lightning came, a shift in the air.

If my fingertips were not placed on the bricks, I would not have remembered the past.

My attention moved to the clouds with the chill against my skin.

I realized I had to enter the unknown.

And for the first time, I was unafraid.

I Defy

Hurts and wounds burden my core.

Turbulent spaces and tangled times cloud my mind.

Cords of lies strangle what I really want to say.

I raise my chest and chin in defiance.

Pisces ♓

Nature – Yin, Water, Mutable
Ruler – Neptune, 12th house
Archetypes – Monk, Mystic, Saint, Dreamer, Martyr

Evolutionary Goals:
- Dissolve illusions
- Develop surrender, consciousness and transcendence
- Unconditional Love

Topics: peace, meditation, solitude, music, myth, fantasy, addiction

Traits: compassionate, forgiving, empathic, imaginative, despairing, escapist, self-destructive, debilitatingly sensitive

Pisces Meditation

I try to separate myself from the insanity of this world and my life in it for some peace.

I try to leave the chaos and confusion I'm stuck in.

But confused and overwhelmed, I feel suffocated as if an entire ocean is swelling from my chest, submerging me completely.

Instead of finding relief at the shore, I'm sucked into the depths and dragged to the ocean's ground amidst sea creatures that look make-believe.

Is this a delusion?

I'm suddenly ecstatic down here. Blissful.

I could wade forever among the reefs here just flowing and Being.

I witness moments of sea nature glistening in the Sunlight even amongst moments of total dullness.

Under the Moonlight, dreary caves and mammals barely alive surpass me everywhere but there is magic in between.

I catch glimpses of what is usually hidden in these majestic forms,

through the mind of a Mystic.

Broken Illusion

In grief, I stare at the
shattered wine glasses of
my past and

mourn for that

illusion that
lulled my thirst for
so long.

Now with nothing
to hold and
nothing to drink,

I reach for the
shards of glass,

reaping more gashes on
my fingers.

At least the pain is real.

Silence

Every thought weighs me down.

But I begin to see the distance words make as
I sit tranquilly on this lotus.

My mind is becoming clear.

I have no struggle, no dilemma.

Nothing.

I am light as a petal.

I am Peace.

Endnote Review Request

If you enjoyed reading this, please leave a review on Amazon.
I read every review and they help new readers discover my
books.

About the Author

Anjali began her journey with evolutionary astrology in 2006 when she learned about her Pluto stellium in the 8th house. Since then, she has plunged into her psyche to uncover inner transformation, self-knowledge, self-empowerment and emotional healing. She provides astrological consultations for individuals and relationships and you can find out more about her at anjalisoi.com.

Printed in France by Amazon
Brétigny-sur-Orge, FR

21157970R00040